Windsor Castle: The History of El

By Charles River Editors

Windsor Castle.

About Charles River Editors

Charles River Editors is a boutique digital publishing company, specializing in bringing history back to life with educational and engaging books on a wide range of topics. Keep up to date with our new and free offerings with this 5 second sign up on our weekly mailing list, and visit Our Kindle Author Page to see other recently published Kindle titles.

We make these books for you and always want to know our readers' opinions, so we encourage you to leave reviews and look forward to publishing new and exciting titles each week.

Introduction

Windsor Castle

"We think of medieval England as being a place of unbelievable cruelty and darkness and superstition. We think of it as all being about fair maidens in castles, and witch-burning, and a belief that the world was flat. Yet all these things are wrong." - Terry Jones

Windsor Castle is one of the most significant residences of the British Monarchy ever conceived, and it has continued to maintain that perfect balance between ancient traditions and modern needs. Built by a conqueror to defend his new domains, it now hosts tourist groups from around the world. The castle has often served as a refuge, with its early battlements offering shelter to royals for centuries, while the castle helped shield others from the attacks of French kings and the Nazis. At the same time, it's known as one of the Royal Family's coziest homes, and it has long been preferred by monarchs with many children, including George III and his famous granddaughter, Victoria. Even today, Queen Elizabeth stays there with four generations of royals, as Prince George and Princess Charlotte scamper across the same lawns that she and her late sister once played on.

Given its importance, it's no surprise Windsor Castle has long been an important national symbol to the English. During the time of the English Civil War, the Puritans held Windsor Castle and used its once beautiful chapel as a prison, but when Charles II came back into power, he turned the castle into a symbol of his dynasty and the permanence he hoped it would enjoy, and though his dynasty did not endure, the castle has.

That said, the buildings themselves have suffered much in their nearly millennium-long history, suffering everything from dry rot to flooding to fire. As recently as 1992, 20% of the castle was destroyed in a fire that began with burning drapes and raged for hours, but each time it looks like the building has finally outlived its usefulness or has been damaged beyond repair, someone comes along, usually someone with a crown or his or her head, and sets it right and restores it. In this way, Windsor Castle, and the British Monarchy, are both likely to last for decades to come.

Windsor Castle: The History of England's Oldest Castle Still In Use examines the long and storied history of one of England's most famous landmarks. Along with pictures depicting important people, places, and events, you will learn about Windsor Castle like never before.

William the Conqueror

William and his half-brothers depicted in the Bayeux Tapestry

The Battle of Hastings is one of history's most famous and important battles, which is why it's widely forgotten that it did not immediately decide the issue of succession to the English throne. In fact, it took William the Conqueror another 10 weeks to finally secure his new crown. During this period, the northern Earls rallied more troops and attempted to put Edgar Aetheling on the throne, and there was resistance when William attempted to cross the Thames at Southwark. In response, he marched right around London, devastating crops and villages as far afield as Middlesex and Hertfordshire. This "harrying of the south" was later eclipsed by events in northern England, but nonetheless it was still very evident in the Domesday survey returns made 20 years later by William's orders.

Eventually, the English sued for peace, and the Earls recognized that it was in their interests to work with William. The nobility swore their loyalty to William, who was crowned William I of England on Christmas Day in 1066.

William had conquered England and remains the last person to successfully invade that nation, but in 1066 he found himself ruling two states separated by 50 miles of wild sea, with plenty of enemies in each. This posed a stiff challenge for any 11th century monarch. William's solution was to establish a team of trusted subordinates in both England and Normandy, and to share his time between the two. In England, the key players were initially William's half-brother, Bishop Odo of Bayeux, who was given significant land holdings in Kent, and Roger of Montgomery, whose stronghold became Sussex. Normandy, as noted earlier, was left with his wife Matilda and his eldest son Robert Curthose.

Both domains would see a series of security threats over the first decade of William's joint rule. William returned to Normandy only five months after Hastings in March 1067, and with him he brought a group of English Earls, including Edwin of Mercier and Morcar of Northumbria, some of whom would prove troublesome later. These were essentially hostages meant to ensure the good behavior of their fellow countrymen, particulalry the remaining noblemen.

In Normandy, matters were relatively stable for the first couple of years, as William's grip on the Norman heartland was firm. When the challenges emerged, they came from familiar quarters, beginning in Maine in 1069. Le Mans revolted, and it was not long before the Anjevins began dabbling in the area, as they had over a decade earlier. The Norman garrison was ejected, and for a time Maine was effectively self-governing itself, something William could not tolerate for long. Unfortunately, William could not take immediate action there because he was engaged in more serious disturbances across the Channel.

Matters worsened in 1070 when William's brother-in-law, Baldwin VI of Flanders, died. There was a dispute over succession, and William Fitz Obern, one of William's most loyal advisors, was killed in a skirmish while attempting to intervene. Robert the Frisian became the Count of Flanders, and although he was also related to William by marriage, his regime was at best frosty towards the Normans. William had lost control of Maine and the security of a firm alliance with Flanders to the north, and to make matters worse, 20 year old King Philip of France was beginning to come of age enough to conspire against William.

With Anjou now openly assisting Maine, the time was ripe for action, but it was not until 1073 that William felt able to lead an army in person in Normandy. He had returned briefly at the end of 1071 in order to reinforce garrisons and issue defensive instructions to his commanders, but what was needed here was a punitive expedition with William at its head. In the summer of 1073, that is precisely what he initiated. His large army, for the first time, was a composite Anglo-Norman force, which was noteworthy given what had been transpiring in England during this same period. That William felt confident enough to lead in person and to assemble such a mixed force was a testament to his self-confidence. The campaign was relatively bloodless and completely successful. Launched against Maine, the rapid capitulation of Le Mans served notice both on Anjou and on the young French King. Maine was brought back under Norman rule, and William's reputation in mainland France was restored. For the time being at least, his hold on Normandy and its borders seemed to be secure.

One reason the use of an Anglo-Norman force was surprising was because William had to spend several years after Hastings struggling to control England. Despite his Christmas coronation, and the flood of loyalty oaths that came with it, William was crowned at a time when he was only truly in control of a fraction of the land. In 1066, England was a heavily divided country, ruled in practice by local noblemen, and though some of them were new blood from Normandy, many of them were figures from the Anglo-Saxon era. Naturally, there was plenty of resentment over Norman rule, and some of the revolts that William had to deal with had a nationalist flavor; but many of these conflicts were simply power struggles between warlords. In military matters, William's approach was always decisive and ruthless, but in the political settlements that followed, he emphasized reconciliation whenever and wherever he could, fully aware that England could not be held down by force of arms alone.

Ironically, the first revolt to disturb the peace in England after William's coronation was a Norman one, beginning with the Count of Boulogne assembling his followers and attacking William's garrison at Dover. Although the attempt ended up being more of a farce than a danger, it only marked the beginning. It was followed by a revolt in Northumbria, which was resolved through diplomacy, and in the west Norman troops had to lay siege to Exeter in 1068 to defuse trouble there as well. While revolts of any type naturally make leaders uneasy, these were small-scale affairs that were relatively easily suppressed or appeased. Indeed, that same year William felt safe enough to bring Matilda across the Channel and have her crowned Queen of England.

In 1069, however, the scale of uprisings entered a new dimension when two of Harold's sons, returned from exile in Ireland, attacked Exeter. Furthermore, in the north a rebelllion coalesced around the figure of Edgar Aethelring, who had been denied the crown in 1066, and his revolt was supported by a Danish invasion. There was trouble at Stafford in the midlands, as well. It was begining to look like 1066 all over again, but this time, with William in the role of Harold.

The Battle of Hastings had been followed by a tempestuous decade that left William constantly worried about security in both of his domains, but he also had to deal with civil matters. Despite the flare-ups, most of the time his subjects lived in relative peace, and William's style was to leave well alone.

As a result, Normandy continued to be governed much as it always had been, and in many ways so did England. The two currencies remained separate, as did the legal systems. England continued to be ruled through its system of local "sherrifs", while Normandy had its "vicomptes", who played similar but not entirely identical roles. English noblemen and churchmen, if they proved loyal, were retained; in fact, Edward the Confessor's Chancellor, Regenbald, served William in the same capacity for years, and an Englishman called Earnwig was appointed Sherrif of Nottingham in 1070. Norman noblemen and close advisors had been rewarded after Hastings with lands seized from Harold's dead courtiers, but even in those cases William allowed the families of the deceased to buy back their ancestral lands.

At the heart of William's administration was commerce. Royal holdings were effectively rented out to whoever could pay the most, allowing them to farm there as they saw fit. The "Danegeld", originally a tax levied to pay for defenses against Viking invaders, continued to be raised most years, and at a high level. Even the criminal law was used to make money; "murdrum", defined by William as the slaying of any Frenchman, resulted in a hefty fine for all of the citizens of the locality concerned. The resulting income to the Crown was not insignificant, an indication that nationalist resentment was still so high that people were willing to pay the price to spill French blood.

In addition to his lightning military campaigns, William sought to exert control by building castles, most consisting of simple log and earth structures that were bolstered with a "moat and bailey." But William also built some heavily fortified stone structures, including Windsor Castle and the Tower of London, and it's estimated that as many as 500 castles of various types were built during William's reign.

The Early History of Windsor Castle

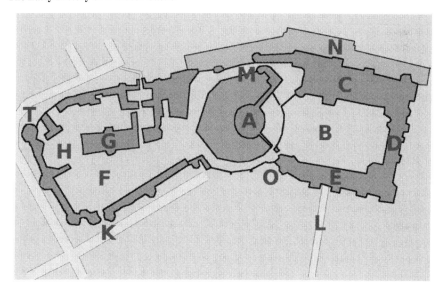

The layout of Windsor Castle:

A: The Round Tower

B: The Upper Ward, The Quadrangle (as this courtyard is known)

C: The State Apartments

D: Private Apartments, overlooking the East terrace

E: South Wing, overlooking The Long Walk

F: Lower Ward

G: St. George's Chapel

H: Horseshoe Cloister

L: The Long Walk

K: King Henry VIII Gate (principal entrance)

M: Norman Gate

N: North Terrace

O: Edward IV Tower

T: The Curfew Tower

R. Sones' picture of the State Apartments

Pictures of the Norman Gate

Petr Noha's picture of the Lower Ward, with (left-right) St George's Chapel, the Lady Chapel, the Round Tower, the lodgings of the Military Knights, and the residence of the Governor of the Military Knights

When work began on Windsor Castle 1076, William intended it to be only one of many such castles located about 20 miles apart and circling London. From the beginning, however, Windsor was special. Located on a high bluff between the River Thames and Windsor Forest, it began as a wooden keep atop an earthen mound called a motte. William, and later his son, added to it, and by the end of the 11th Century, it was a sizeable establishment featuring three wooden baileys. These, along with the keep, formed a rough outline of the shape of the current castle.

For all the work they put into it, neither William nor his son had any intention of living at Windsor Castle. Instead, Henry I moved into the completed castle in 1110, and later, in 1121, he married his wife Adela there. It is difficult to imagine what the new queen thought of her home, for it was during this time that the original keep began to collapse. After shoring it up with timbers, Henry finally ordered a low wall built around it to keep it from giving way any further.

A medieval depiction of Henry I

Henry I seemed only interested in keeping what was already built standing and so it remained for his grandson, Henry II to add more to the castle. Between 1165 and 1179, he used the latest technology of the time to replace many of the wooden structures with stone ones, and he also added well-spaced towers that would allow his men a better vantage point from which to spot attacking forces. He reduced the keep in size and shored up the foundations on the south side of the fortress, but he also updated the royal apartments to make them more comfortable for himself and his family.

Upon ascending to the throne, Henry II's son, King John, continued these improvements. John did not feel the need for any significant additions to the castle's fortifications, something he may have regretted when his own barons revolted against him and besieged the castle in 1214 and

1216. The first siege helped lead to the signing of the Magna Carta at nearby Runnymede.

A contemporary depiction of John

Learning from his predecessor's mistakes, Henry III threw himself into improving and strengthening the castle's defenses, adding, among other things, three more towers. The work was not cheap, as an account from the era shows: "Ralph Tirel constable of Windsor. William of Staines received for him an account of £413 and half a mark (6s. 8d.) which he received from the King's treasury for the works of the Castle of Windsor from the Purification of the Blessed Mary of the eighth year (2nd February, 1223-4), when Hubert of Burgh the justiciar received the Castle into his custody, until the Saturday next before the feast of St. Dunstan of the ninth year (17th May 1225)…In the treasury, nothing. And in the work of the same castle and of the houses in the castle for the same time £413 6s. 8d. by the King's writ and by view of Richard and Robert of

Shaw as is contained in a roll of particulars which they delivered into the treasury. And they are quit."

While fortifications were important to Henry III, he did not neglect his own comfort, nor that of his bride, Eleanor of Provence, whom he married in 1236. Windsor was one of his favorite homes, and he wanted a special place in which to live with his wife and children. Thus, a few years later, he sent the following order to Walter of Burgh: "We command you that in the Castle of Windsor you cause to be made a certain lodging [camera) for our use near the wall of the same Castle, 60 feet long and 28 feet wide, and another lodging for the use of our Queen, 40 feet long, which is to be joined to our lodging and be under the same roof along the same wall, and a certain chapel, 70 feet long and 28 feet wide, along the same wall. So that a certain sufficient space be left between the aforesaid lodgings and the chapel itself to make a certain grassplat."

Later, on June 10, 1241, Henry sent a message, "Concerning many things in the Castle of Windsor…to his beloved and faithful Engelard of Cygony…" Part of it read, "We command you that since it was ordained by our beloved uncle Peter of Savoy by the advice of Hugh Giffard as well as yourself that no horse be left within the walls of our Castle of Windsor until at least the months of August and September next have passed, and that you take it not ill that in the meantime your horses be amoved. Adhering to their and your advice we will and order it to be done because we shall be in every way content that within the aforesaid Castle you should take them out as soon as the rainy weather comes. We will also that as you have arranged between you, your kitchen be amoved and rebuilt in the place appointed."

While it is difficult to decipher exactly why the king would issue such an order, it seems quite possible that the presence of horses, or more specifically their excrement, was making the castle rather unpleasant during the hot summer months, especially when it rained. The kitchen he wanted moved so that it would be closer to the Upper Ward, and therefore more convenient for family meals.

Henry was intent that his personal apartments be as beautiful and stylish as possible, and to that end he ordered on November 24, 1243, "We command you that by day and by night you cause the high chamber above the wall of the Castle near our chapel in the upper bailey of the Castle to be wainscoted; so that it may be ready and decently wainscoted by this Friday when we shall come thither, namely with boards rayed and coloured, and that nothing reprehensible may be found in that wainscoting." He then added, "You are also to have made in each gable of the same chamber a white glass window outside the inner window of each gable, so that when the inner windows have been opened those glass windows may appear outside."

Henry's bedroom and the chambers for his other family members were located in the part of the castle known as the Upper Ward, along with the beautiful Lady Chapel, one of the largest of its kind in the nation. On August 20, 1243, the king ordered, "The archbishop of York is enjoined to cause work to go on both in winter and in summer till the King's chapel of Windsor be finished, and to have a high wooden roof made in the same after the manner of the roof of the new work of Lichfield, so that the stone work may be seen, with good wainscoting and painting, and to cause that chapel to be covered with lead, and four gilt images to be fashioned in the same chapel and to be set in the places which the King had beforehand arranged for them to be put, and a stone turret at the front of the same chapel in which may be hung three or four bells." This portion of the castle was intended to be more private, and withdrawn from the rest of the area, while the Lower Ward would serve as a place to carry out public duties.

As was the practice of the day, the king and his court would not only have their own chapel but also their own chaplain, and it was considered important that the man of God have a comfortable place to live. To that end, Henry ordered in 1260, "Because we will that the venerable father A[ustin], bishop of Laodicea, do inhabit the houses opposite our chapel of Windsor in which our domestic chaplains and our clerks of our chapel have been accustomed to lie: we order you to cause those houses to be repaired with what necessary repair they need, and on the soil of those houses you have made a certain chimney de plastro franco, and between those houses and the chapel aforesaid a certain gate with a wicket."

Even a king has limited resources, so Henry kept a close eye on the cost of his building projects. On November 23, 1252, the following order went out: "Because there are many more workmen in the Castle of Windsor than is necessary, from whose works by reason of the shortness of the days of this present time the King derives…profit, the King wills that the greater part of them be discharged, together with the painters who are in the same Castle, whom the King wills to cease from their works for a season since they cannot work properly by reason of the dampness of winter time." Henry III had good reason to be concerned about the costs of the painters he employed, for these were not just ordinary men but artists hired to add various religious murals to the castle's new and existing walls.

At the same time, a castle was much more than just a beautiful and comfortable home for the king; it was also a place of refuge in case of attack, and in a time of siege, nothing was more important for those wanting to avoid surrender than a good source of water. Henry knew this well enough that in May, 1256 he ordered Godfrey of Liston that "from the outgoings of your bailiwick you cause to be mended the defects of the masonry on the top of the great tower of Windsor Castle, and that you cause the water of the well in the court beside the aforesaid tower to be led as far as our cloister in the lower court, and thence to the door of our hall…if the water of the aforesaid well be not sufficient, you are to cause the water of the well in the great tower to be taken to the help of the other water, and you are to cause a house to be made anew over the aforesaid well, with a wheel and other engines, and a certain lavatory at the head of our hall on the east side." Henry's men did such a good job that the well they built remained in use in the 20th century.

Sadly, the Great Hall that Henry worked so hard on was lost to a fire in 1296, and his successor, Edward I, chose not to rebuild it. In fact, very little was done on the castle until the reign of Edward III. Born in one of Windsor Castle's many bedrooms, Edward felt a special affinity for it, so much so that in September 1327, just months after he ascended the throne, he ordered a survey done on the castle to determine what work would be needed to make it comfortable to live in again. This survey found, among other things:

> "[T]here are seven bridges in the aforesaid Castle, of which four are drawbridges and are very weak and much need to be mended"

> "[T]wo towers between the great gate and the Clewer tower (which towers at some time were finished off with wooden tables), by divers storms they are rotten and prostrate"

> "[T]he glass windows of the great chapel are much broken and rent by strong winds and divers other storms, and much need to be mended as to iron and glass"

> "[T]here is a...turret in the same place behind our lady the Queen's kitchen which is much rent, and in many parts damaged from top to bottom, and especially in three places, and it must be mended quickly with quarry stone with fiting work"

> "[T]here are lacking three great hempen cables for three wells, and for cleaning the said three wells by reckoning and mending of the wheels of the said wells"

> "[T]here is a certain tower in which is the lodging of the Queen's seneschal in the upper bailey, and in the same places are many defects through divers fractures and cracks in the stone wall, and through false gutters"

> "[T]he Queen's great kitchen in the upper bailey, together with a larder on one part and a great bakehouse on the other in the same place, much...are weakened, especially on account of the failure of the timber and because they were not covered for a long time.... Also another outer wall above the latrine of the lodging over the gate beside the high tower is much damaged and by divers tempests...."

Chivalry and the power of the crown were both very important to Edward, and he was determined to make Windsor a symbol of both. To this end, he announced in 1344 that "we have appointed our beloved William of Hurley, our carpenter, to choose by himself or his deputies, as many carpenters in the cities, towns, and other places of our kingdom of England, both within their liberties and without, wherever they can be found, as he may need for certain works which we have appointed to be done in our Castle of Windsor, and to bring them to the aforesaid Castle as quickly as he can, there to remain at our wages on the aforesaid works."

A posthumous depiction of Edward III

Edward III had good reason to be interested in the castle's condition, because in 1344 he decided to make it the headquarters in the Upper Ward for his new Order of the Round Table. In addition to the repairs being made, Edward ordered a new building built within the castle walls to provide a special space for his new organization to meet in. In his 14th century *Chronicon Anglice*, Thomas of Walsingham recorded that in 1344, "King Edward caused many workmen to be summoned to the Castle of Windsor and began to build a house which should be called the Round Table. Its area had from the centre to the circumference through the semi-diameter 100 feet, and so its diameter was 200 feet. The expenses by the week were at first £100, but afterwards, on account of the news which the King received from France, they were curtailed to £20, because he decided that much treasure must be got together for other affairs."

Unfortunately, the Order of the Round Table never took off; as Edward was beginning to form it, the dreadful Black Death was beginning its spread across Europe, reaching England in 1348. He had to stop all work on his castle, as men were afraid to leave their homes and farms to interact with others. Two years passed before the plaque, which took the lives of nearly half the country's population, finally ended and Edward was able to get back to his building project. On April 26, he ordered his men "to take and provide masons, carpenters, and other workmen who may be needed for our works aforesaid, wherever they can be found, within the liberties and outside the fee of the Church only excepted, and except the workmen already retained for our works at Westminster, our Tower of London, and Dartford; also to take and provide stone, timber, and other necessaries for the works aforesaid, and carriage for the same timber and stone and other premises; and to bring back those workmen who were retained for our works in the said Castle of Windsor and have withdrawn from the same works without our licence..."

In the years that had passed, many of the supplies that Edward had gathered for the project had disappeared, and while he was not inclined to prosecute those who had taken them during that desperate time, he was anxious to have them back. Thus, he ordered his men "to enquire by the oath of upright and lawful men of every county of our realm of England, through whom the. truth oi the matter can the better be known, if the timber or stone bought and provided for our works has in any wise been carried off or removed, and to cause the same timber and stone so removed, wherever it can be found to be brought back..."

Edward knew that the project would have to be funded, and to that end he told those under him "to buy and provide all things needful for our works aforesaid; and to sell the boughs and other residues of the trees provided for our works for our service and answer to us for the moneys arising therefrom; receiving for his own wages twelve pence a day while he abides there, and two shillings a day when he shall be intent upon our business elsewhere, and three shillings a week for the wages of his clerk." This project was not just an act of personal pride but also an excellent way to restart an economy that was driven to a standstill by the plague.

In another move to bolster morale, he founded the Order of the Garter and the Poor Knights of Windsor. The latter was an organization of knights who had lost their estates in service to the king and therefore were granted housing inside Windsor Castle.

On October 31, 1356, the king named William of Wykeham to oversee the work being done on the castle. According to one contemporary account, "the King has appointed the same William surveyor of the aforesaid works; also to engage and provide masons, carpenters and other workmen whatsover, and also stone, timber, and all other things necessary for those works, and carriage for the same timber and stone and other things set forth by the same William or those deputed by him for the King's monies to be paid thereupon..." Furthermore, William was "to arrange for the wages for the workmen in the Castle and park aforesaid by view made of Richard of Taynton, John the painter, and Ralph of Dodlesfold, or two of them, and to buy and provide all things necessary for the aforesaid works, and to sell the branches and other residues from the trees provided for those works for the King's use, and to answer for the sums arising thence to the King...." Finally, he was authorized to command "the barons to reckon with the aforesaid William of the wages outgoings costs and expenses which the same William reasonably rendered and applied by view and testimony of the aforesaid Richard, John and Ralph, or two of them..."

Among the items Wykeham purchased during his first year in charge were the following:

"1917 lbs. of iron, 6500 leadnails, 5000 great spikings, 26100 "second spikings," 3101 quarters of nails with tinned heads, 30000 roofnails, 11000 lITle nails, 58700 traversnails, 500 great nails and 1000 boardnails"

"373 loads of stones from Reigate quarry, 54 stones from the Wheatley quarry, and 1515 scappled heath stones bought of divers people at divers prices...."

"41000 tiles for pavements, 16000 roofing tiles, 37 hollow tiles...."

"131 lbs. of tin...49 rings, 79 latches, 44 pairs of vertivels with crooks and 12 slots, 61 locks and 68 keys...."

"93 long and transverse irons for windows in the High tower;"

Looking back on Wykeham's work, chronicler Ranulf Higden observed in his *Polychonicon*, "About the year of our Lord 1359 our lord the King, at the instance of William Wikham, clerk, caused many excellent buildings in the Castle of Windsor to be thrown down, and others more fair and sumptuous to be set up. For almost all the masons and carpenters throughout the whole of England were brought to that building, so that hardly anyone could have any good mason or carpenter, except in secret, on account of the King's prohibition...Moreover, the said William Wikham was of very low birth, he was even reported to be of servile condition, yet he was very shrewd, and a man of great industry. Considering how he could please the King and secure his goodwill, he counselled the King to build the said Castle of Windsor in such wise as appears today to the beholder." Whatever others may have thought of Wykeham, Edward trusted him but still remained at the castle to supervise the work, living in the cramped quarters of the Round Tower during this time.

When the project was completed, those approaching Windsor Castle would be struck by the tall roofline of the new range towering over the rest of the castle. Those entering from the front would pass through between the Kitchen and the Spicerie Gatehouses into St. George's Hall, a newly built structure that also housed a new, semi-public chapel. They would no doubt be impressed by the rows of large windows that looked out on the three large courts lined up to the north of the Upper Ward. These were known as the Little Cloister, the King's Cloister and the Kitchen Court, respectively. Those who were close friends of the King would be admitted into the Rose Tower, in the west corner, while those visiting other members of his court would turn toward the east, where well designed and furnished rooms would greet them. Edward also had some work done on the Lower Ward, enlarging the chapel and other buildings in that section. He also installed a large, weight-driven clock in the Round Tower, the first of its kind to be used in England.

In addition to working on repairing and improving Windsor, Wykeham also oversaw furnishing it and adding to its already existing furnishings. He reported purchasing, among other things, the following for Edward's own use:

"a bench, 2 andirons, an iron fork for the King's first chamber.

a bench, 2 andirons, an iron fork for the King's second chamber.

a bench, and a stool for the King's closet.

2 benches, 2 stools, 2 great desks, a little desk for the King's chapel.

2 tables, 3 benches, 2 pair of trestles, an iron fork for the King's third chamber.

5 benches, 2 screens, 2 andirons, an iron fork, 10 stools for the King's fourth chamber.

a bench, 2 andirons, an iron fork for the King's fifth chamber called La Rose.

2 benches, 2 andirons, a fork, a table, a pair of trestles for the King's painted chamber.

...3 pairs of steps for the King's chambers."

The Queen, Philippa of Hainault, whom Edward had married in 1328, and who had given him 13 children, was far from forgotten. Among the items purchased for her use were the following:

"a screen, 2 little tables, 2 andirons for the Queen's first chamber.

a table, a bench, a cupboard, 3 stools, 2 trestles, 2 great trestles for carrying the altar for the Queen's

second chamber with the little chapel.

2 tables, 2 benches for the door of the Queen's chamber."

Wykeham also bought items for the public areas of the castle, including:

"a table with feet, a bench at the door for the usher of the hall

"4 tables, 6 benches, 11 trestles, a great iron fork, an iron shovel for the great chamber"

"…a table, 2 benches at the door of the great chamber for the usher."

"5 tables, 6 pair of trestles, 6 benches for the chamber with mirrors.

6 tables, 6 benches, 5 pairs of steps, 7 pair of trestles pour la daunsyng chamber (the dancing chamber).

3 tables, 4 trestles, a cupboard for the dais in the hall.

11 tables, 4 benches, 11 pair of trestles for the same hall.

5 tables, 13 benches for the cloister"

In all, Edward III spent £51,000 on his great building project, which would be a large sum in modern money but was unheard of during his lifetime. In fact, the work he did on Windsor Castle remained the single largest expenditure in English history during the Middle Ages. With an average annual income of only £30,000, he had to be creative in raising funds for his efforts, including ransoming French prisoners of war following various English victories. Among those held was King John II of France. Needless to say, his ransom paid for some very expensive windows and walls.

King John II of France

A New Era

Edward III died in 1377 and was succeeded by his grandson, Richard II, who found the castle sufficiently comfortable and did very little work on it except for restoring the area that now houses St. George's Chapel (at that time it was the Mother Church of the Order of the Garter). Supervising this work was his Clerk of Works, an aspiring young writer named Geoffrey Chaucer. Chaucer would go on to complete a number of building projects for Richard, though no others at Windsor.

Chaucer

In addition to the fact that the castle was already in excellent condition when he inherited it, Richard had another good reasons were not focusing a great deal of attention on his home; his reign was marked by a growing unrest in the country. In 1399 Henry IV, Richard's cousin, led an uprising against him and captured Windsor and the crown. He was only marginally interested in the former, but he did complain to Parliament in January 1404 about "how the castles and other of the King's manors are very ruinous, and in need of great renewal and reparation, and how the profits of them are given to divers persons, and the King bears the charges; and above all the Castle of Windsor, to which there was assigned a certain fund for its reparation, and now the same fund is given to certain persons, and the King bears the charges."

Though he was very much a man of war, Henry did hold the church in high esteem too, and in 1409 he authorized spending "because…the warden and canons of our free chapel within the Castle of Windsor are not fully endowed as to houses and lodgings for their vicars, clerks, choristers, and servants, as we have understood, we have granted to the same dean and canons a certain vacant place within our Castle aforesaid called Woodhaw, beside the great hall…" They were "to build there houses for the vicars, clerks, and choristers aforesaid; to have and to hold the aforesaid place to them and their successors forever…And we have likewise given leave to the same warden and canons to receive the place aforesaid from us and to build houses and lodgings there as is aforesaid, and that they can hold those so built for themselves and their successors forever as is aforesaid by tenor of these presents, the Statute of Mortmain notwithstanding."

Henry reigned only 14 years and died a young man, leaving his crown and Windsor to his oldest son, Henry V, who also did little in the way of improvements. In fact, as the Wars of the Roses raged between 1455 and 1485, the various monarchs ruling had little time or interest in Windsor, even though it saw the birth of England's youngest king, Henry VI, who was born in December 1421 and ascended to the throne the following year.

It was not until the time of Edward IV that work again began on the castle. In 1475, Edward ordered that several of the older, more worn down structures located in the Lower Ward be torn down so that he could build a new, larger, and more elaborate church. Known today as St. George's Chapel, Edward saw it as a symbol of his family's future on the English throne. However, in spite of his efforts, his reign soon ended, and two years later, so did his dreams of a family dynasty; the House of Tudor took control of the throne in 1485, when Henry VII began his reign.

Andrew K. Brook's picture of St. George's Chapel

Josep Renalias' picture of the interior of St. George's Chapel

Like his more notorious son, Henry VII enjoyed a good feast and a comfortable living, and he used Windsor extensively for both. Finding the castle already to his liking, he made few changes, focusing most of his attention on converting the exquisite Lady Chapel into one in honor of his ancestor, Henry VI, who at that time was being considered for sainthood. Henry's hopes for the latter were never fulfilled, which led to him losing interest in the former. He also did some maintenance type work on his own apartments, including having a new roof put on the Great Kitchen and adding a three-storied tower that he could use for his private living area.

Henry VIII is well known for being more interested in women than wainscoting and therefore made few changes to Windsor. He grew up there as a young man and threw a number of lavish entertainments there from time to time, but he preferred to keep Hampton Court as his primary residence. Nevertheless, in 1510 he had extensive work done on the main gate that led into the castle, as chronicler Leland noted: "Henry VIII, the flower of Kings…in the first years of his reign he built from the foundations, of squared stone, the great gate, by which there is the entry into the area of the first castle." Another contemporary wrote, "King Ren. VIII. made the Porter's Lodge, or first Gate, as you enter into the Castle, which is called the Exchequer, wherein the Courte, and Records of the Honour be kept and holden."

Lewis Clarke's picture of the Henry VIII Gate

Henry VIII

An avid tennis player in his youth, Henry built a court just at the base of the motte on which
the Upper Ward stood. He also built the North Wharf on the outer wall of the Upper Ward,
where he could sit in the afternoons and watch the River Thames flow by. According to Sir
William Henry St. John Hope, "The works upon the new wharf were begun...on 18th May,
1533, and continued...for two years.... Throughout the...second year's account all the workmen
at the Castle were engaged upon the new wharf. The bricklayers are described as making brick
vaults under the said wharf to carry off the water from the Castle leads, building buttresses and
underpinning the ground plates and spurs with brick, and in making brick benches along the new
walk. The carpenters continued framing and setting up the railing, laying planks for the brick
drains and making sluices under the walk, and covering the brick benches with boarding...By the
summer of 1534 the work had extended as far westwards as the wall that marked the boundary of
the dean and canons, which was raised and repaired, and a doorway made in it. Early in the new
year the carpenters had finished their work, and the new walk was handed over to the labourers
to level and put in order.... The whole was finally completed in September by the finishing of

the brick buttresses." And what did it look like? Hope explained, "…the "new wharf ' was a terrace, built out upon wooden spurs and edged with a wooden railing, extending along the whole of the north front of the upper bailey to the canons' boundary wall. Beyond this was a continuation of the railing as far as the hundred steps and a flight of steps down to the college garden. At the east end was a wooden bridge across the Castle ditch into the park."

Colin Smith's picture of the Thames and Windsor Castle in the background

Later, in June 1533, one author recalled that nine plasterers were "working as well upon whiting the roof, walls and chimneys off all the new lodgings called the prince's lodging as also the roof and walls off the entry between the Kings Great Chamber and the said new lodging as also not only whiting the walls of the chamber called the Sedge off Rodys but also yellow ochering the roof and windows off the same. Moreover not only whiting the walls off the king's bed chamber and the entry between the Roods Chamber and the King's Closet and plastering and whiting the King's stool chamber but also yellow ochering the King's bed chamber."

A few years later, when some nobles rose up against him in 1536, Henry shut himself up in Windsor and used the castle as a base of operations to defeat them. Likewise, he occasionally headed to Windsor when the plague struck London and Hampton Court was considered too close for comfort.

The other massive project undertaken during Henry's reign was the restyling of the Lady Chapel into a mausoleum for Cardinal Wolsey, who had once been a favorite adviser of the king, but the two had a falling out before the famous Italian architect and sculptor, Benedetto Grazzini, could finish his changes. As a result, Henry took the chapel back for himself, but even when he was finally interred there in 1547, the chapel remained unfinished.

Edward VI, Henry's much longed-for son, came to the throne upon his father's death and soon made it clear that he had no interest in improving anything about Windsor. Raised in the harsh traditions of the early Protestant Reformation, he eschewed frivolity and ceremony, preferring to live simply in plainer surroundings. The only time he made significant use of the castle was in 1549, when problems with his subjects drove him to take refuge in the castle until the issues could be resolved. Even then, he complained, "Methink I am in a prison, here are no galleries, nor no gardens to walk in".

Edward would die in his teens and be succeeded by his older sister, Mary I. Notoriously known today as Bloody Mary, she did not share her brother's disdain for elegance and comfort, but she still demanded that she and her court live a spiritually rigorous and physically limited life. That said, she did make use of the some of the money and goods her father and brother had taken from broken-up abbeys to build a fountain in the Upper Ward. Work on it included "painting and gilding one great vane with the King and Queen's Arms with a great Imperial Crown upon it all gilt with fine Gold and painted with fine oil colors. ... painting…gilding and varnishing of a great Lion and one Eagle holding up the said vane…one Gryffon, a harte, a Greyhound and an Antilope holding up four Compartments with 4 Badges Crowned within them…."

Mary also ordered more housing built for the increasing number of Knights of Windsor who requested to live there, but that was the extent of her efforts during her brief, tumultuous reign. By the time her sister, Elizabeth I, came to the throne, the Marquess of Winchester wrote to Sir William Cecil in June 1559, "And forget not the articles of my last letter written to you I pray you for reparations must needs be done at Windsor by me or some other man before the queen's might come there, assuring you there is much work to be done about the terrace for the queen's going into the Park where her highness must needs make her walk." Two months later, he added, "the Castle is ready for the queen's living for this time, albeit in searching of the Castle much of the principal timber is utterly decayed and must be amended this next year, or it will not continue and that I mind shall be done. ... And there is lacking to make the Castle dry at this time, fodder of lead, which must be bought or taken of the queen's store out of the tower where rests…fodder that was gathered together this last year from the bulwarks of Gravesend…. , thinking best the queen's might write her letter to the lieutenant to deliver the…fodder of it while the workmen be there…."

Contemporary historian William Lambarde wrote in 1577 that "about the 17th Year of her most happy Reign, she began with the Castle itself also, and not only restored throughout the ruinous Parts thereof to their former Strength and Integrity, but also converted four sundry Bridges, and a Terrace of decayed Timber into so many new Works of beautiful Stone, adding besides a faire

Stone Gate at the rubbish Gate, and a most gorgeous Chapel within the Palace itself; Things not less profitable for Use, then pleasant for the Eye."

Elizabeth, who understood better than most how precarious power could be, preferred to stay at Windsor because it was easily defended. While she was primarily interested in it martial potential – she even added 10 state-of-the-art brass cannons to its already formidable defenses - she also made some minor improvements to its buildings. Perhaps remembering a few happy walks with her late father, she added some statuary and carvings to the North Wharf, and she built a large eight-sided building on it in which she could hold banquets and other entertainments. She enjoyed entertaining at the castle, something William Shakespeare himself observed in *The Merry Wives of Windsor*, when Mistress Quickly cries:

> "About, about;
> Search Windsor Castle, elves, within and out:
> Strew good luck, ouphes, on every sacred room:
> That it may stand till the perpetual doom,
> In state as wholesome as in state 'tis fit,
> Worthy the owner, and the owner it.
> The several chairs of order look you scour
> With juice of balm and every precious flower:
> Each fair instalment, coat, and several crest,
> With loyal blazon, evermore be blest!
> And nightly, meadow-fairies, look you sing,
> Like to the Garter's compass, in a ring:
> The expressure that it bears, green let it be,
> More fertile-fresh than all the field to see;
> And 'Honi soit qui mal y pense' write
> In emerald tufts, flowers purple, blue and white;
> Let sapphire, pearl and rich embroidery,
> Buckled below fair knighthood's bending knee:
> Fairies use flowers for their charactery.
> Away; disperse: but till 'tis one o'clock,
> Our dance of custom round about the oak
> Of Herne the hunter, let us not forget."

Queen Elizabeth

Like his predecessor, King James I treated Windsor primarily as a center of entertainment, usually in the form of hunting and drinking, whereas Charles I preferred more intellectual pursuits and spent much time and money on improving those aspects over the aesthetics of the castle, particularly St. George's Chapel and the gateway leading to the North Terrace.

Unfortunately, many of the items Charles I and others had purchased to adorn the chapel and other rooms of the castle fell into the hand of the parliamentarians during the English Civil War and were never found. In addition to executing Charles I, the parliamentarians turned the castle into something of a prison, throwing out those who lived there and turning the beautiful Lady Chapel into a magazine in which to store guns and powder.

Restoration

Lord Protector Oliver Cromwell and the Puritans remained uninterested in the castle as anything other than a military base, so it was not until Charles II was restored to the throne that any improvements were made on it. By that time, according to an 1880 account written by William Dixon, "The King's house was a wreck; the fanatic, the pilferer, and the squatter, having been at work. Elizabeth's theatre was gone; the private chapel was stripped of its sacred furnishings; hall and gallery were spoiled; St. George's hall being stripped of its knightly shields, the king's gallery of its cabinets and works of art. Tudor tower and secret room were closed. Paupers had squatted in many of the towers and cabinets...Outside, the ruin was no less complete. The stand and rails were broken down. Much of the had been taken up. ... The keeper's lodge, close by Elizabeth's walk, had been destroyed...St. George's choir was closed.... Dean, canons, choristers, knew their places on the hill no more. The altars were defaced, the hatchments overturned, the communion-table carted off. ... Not only was the shrine dismantled, but the saint himself was stricken from the calendar. No other saints were tolerated save the saints of God. Except his cross, nothing of the saint was spared; the barred white flag of Sluys and Aginourt; which floated from the keep — less as an emblem of the cross than of the sword."

Charles II

Charles would not give up on the old castle, seeing it perhaps as a symbol of all he was trying to restore to the nation. He made Prince Rupert, he own kinsman, the Constable of Windsor Castle and mostly gave him a free hand in repairing and modernizing both the private and public spaces. In 1676, Charles II ordered that "where as we did think fit for the enlarging of our Terrace walk of Windsor Castle to take in the Colligate walk belonging to the Deane and Cannons of our Royall Chapel there... and whereas we did... signify to them by... our works of our said Castle that our intention was that in consideration of their Collegiate walk so taken in they and their successors should have the free use of our said Terrace walk with full liberty to enter in with their one Keys and their to walk at all times we have thought fit in Pursuance of our said promise to them hereby to signify the same to you...... our Pleasure that you permit and suffer the said Deane and Canons and their successors from time to time freely to enter with their one Keys, which we are Pleased they should have for that Purpose, into our said Terrace walk and their to walk at all times and our Pleasure is also that is our Royall Declaration in this behalf be registered in the register of our said Church."

The work Charles authorized showed his interest in the French court of his rival, Louis XIV, the famed Sun King. Charles hired architects Hugh May and others to recreate what that architect found in Paris, and the result was what one author called "the most extravagantly Baroque interiors ever executed in England," including one building with rows and rows of carefully aligned rooms in the enfilade style popular then. This new structure was called the Star Building in honor of the large star Charles hung on its side. Diarist John Evelyn noted on June 16, 1683, "That which was new at Windsor since I was last there, and was surprising to me, was the incomparable fresco painting in St George's Hall, representing the legend of St. George, and triumph of the Black Prince, and his reception by Edward III.; the volto, or roof, not totally finished; then the Resurrection in the Chapel, where the figure of the Ascension is, in my opinion, comparable to any paintings of the most famous Roman masters; the Last Supper, also over the altar... I liked the contrivance of the unseen organ behind the altar, nor less the stupendous and beyond all description the incomparable carving of our Gibbon, who is, without controversy, the greatest master both for invention and rareness of work, that the world ever had in any age; nor doubt I at all that he will prove as great a master in the statuary art."

May

Charles's successor, James II, ruled for only a few short, tumultuous years, so it remained for William III to make the next major improvements to the castle. He hired Sir Christopher Wren to remodel the Upper Ward in a more classical style, but William died young, also, so it fell on Queen Anne to continue the work. 19th Century architect Ambrose Poynter later wrote, "The talents of Sir C. Wren were called upon for a design to convert the Castle, as far as might be practicable, into a regular edifice, and to connect with it an extensive and magnificent suite of gardens. By the plan of this eminent architect, it was proposed to take down the greater part of the South side of the upper ward, in order to make room for a new building of about two hundred feet frontage, with a gateway in the middle...To this as a centre, the remainder of the old building Eastward would have formed a wing, and a corresponding wing to the Westward would have completed a front of about five hundred feet, central to the Long Walk, and symmetrical in its form, though not very consistent in its style, since the centre...would have been in the Italian taste, and the existing wing...was to be nearly what it had been made in the time of Charles II...Between the principal entrance on the South side and the Long Walk was designed an Italian garden, laid out on different levels, connected by flights of steps. On the North side, a double ramp from the terrace opposite the Star building would have led down to a lower terrace, and thence to a garden in the same style, reaching to the river, and occupying the whole of that side of the Little Park, with an ornamental canal and jets-d'eau down the centre. From this garden a third branched off at a right angle and extended Eastward."

Wren

Darren Smith's picture of the Long Walk

Anne was more interested in what lay outdoors than inside, and the early 18th century saw some rather extensive work done on the gardens surrounding the castle. Henry Evans, the gardener, was paid "for Work done in the little and Great Parks at Windsor, by planting of Trees in Busshey Grounds in the little Park and Day Work done there in sowing Hay Seed where wanted, also making into Slopes and Levels the Ground where the Cockpit, Chocolate, and other old Houses stood, sloping, levelling and turfing the Castle Ditch, by the Park Gate and repairing the new Road on the outside of the said Park Wall that was damaged by the overflowing of the Thames, also putting into Order the new Road in the Great Park that was damaged by the Wetness of the Weather"

Furthermore, he was in charge of "putting it into Order to answer to those Lines of Palisades, carting of Earth and raising the Ground on the Slopes that lay to settle all the Summer, working it to its Lines and Levels and sowing all with Hay Seed, in binding the Trees in the several Walks, Avenues and Plantations in the two Parks, in mowing the several new made Slopes, and those formerly made on the North and South Sides of the Castle, and also the Piece of Ground where the Cockpit stood that is sown with Hay Seed, planting, cupping, mulching, and watering the Hill adjoining to the Keepers Lodge, also digging of Graved in Order to new lay the Great Court Yard and Terrace Walk."

Anne's successors, the patriarchs of the House of Hanover, generally preferred the other palaces and estates and largely ignored Windsor Castle. However, in the mid-18th Century, the empty castle became something of a tourist attraction, with middle class peoplepaying the castle keeper to wander around the halls and see the oddities that generations of royalty had acquired. In 1753, George Bickham published the first guidebook to the castle, and after describing the buildings, he wrote, "[W]e shall now conduct our Readers into the Park, which lies, contiguous, and is kept as smooth as a Carpet. … To conclude, all the Parks about Wind for are very agreeable and spacicus. Even the Little Park (as it is generally called) is at least three Miles in Circumference: The great one Fourteen, and the Forest above Thirty…The first is peculiar to the Court; the others are open and free for Riding, Hunting, or taking the Air, according as the Gentlemen, or Ladies who reside in the Parts adjacent, are respectively disposed. In a Word, the Lodges in these Parks, which have been beautified by their respective Rangers, might, with Propriety enough, be called Palaces, were not their Glory eclipsed by the Palace itself, to which they belong."

King George III, with his large family and eccentric ways, did not care to live at Hampton Court but instead chose to make his home at Windsor, where he could enjoy the grounds. After settling into the Upper Lodge in the early 1760s, he allowed the villagers and even some tourists to continue to wonder around the grounds. As time went on, however, he put more and more work into its rooms, and he began to limit outside access to his home.

George III

George hired James Wyatt to, in the words of one author, "transform the exterior of the buildings in the Upper Ward into a Gothic palace, while retaining the character of the Hugh May state rooms." He ordered the building's exterior to be made reminiscent of its Gothic past, with additional turrets and strong new battlements. During this period, one author, Pyne, described the public areas of the castle: "This grand approach to the state apartments is situated in the north angle of the upper ward, and includes a porch leading to a vestibule divided by a centre and two sides, vaulted in a style of rich Gothic. From this porch to the commencement of the stairs is forty-five feet, the centre division is fourteen, and the sides each seven feet wide; their extent one hundred and eight feet... in these are niches with Gothic canopies of tabernacle-work. The stairs are divided into two flights, the first of nineteen, the second of fifteen steps. There is a gallery in front, and one on each side; the front gallery is twenty-eight feet in length, the side galleries each forty-seven feet. The balustrades to the stair case and galleries are elegantly designed, and executed in iron bronzed, with bases and capitals of burnished brass."

Modern History

Mark S. Jobling's aerial photo of Windsor Castle

In the early 1800s, Edward Wyatt, a carver, was hired to execute a number of projects, one of the most ambitious being to create a "rich Frize [sic] for the Queens Audience Chamber Emblematically describing two of the Elements, Land and Water, the produce of each in a Cornucopia, the shamrock and the rose, represent the Union Crowning the shield in the Center which is supported by the Lion Couched on the Faisceau d'Armes (Emblem of Force)." Furthermore, "The City Shield is introduced on the right bound to the Anchor by a Crown of Laurels, with emblems of Commerce and the Sword & Scales of Justice. The most noble Order of the Garter supported by the Oak (to imply strength) the Bath to the Laurels (of Victory) The Medals in the Cornucopia are rewards His Majesty presents to his most deserving Subjects An Oak Frame for dITo to form Pannels, & fixing the above at Windsor."

George III spent the last years of his life confined at Windsor, suffering from dementia likely caused by porphyria. He died in 1820 and was succeeded by his son, George IV, who had already authorized the size of the Royal Lodge increased and subsequently began working on updating the facilities at Windsor. He even convinced Parliament to authorize him to spend £300,000 on the work, and he hired Jeffry Wyatville to begin in 1824.

In June 1830 Wyatville reported what had been done:

"Twelve old houses have been pulled down and cleared away.

The boundary-wall to the round tower-mound on the east has been built.

The new Saint George's gate and adjoining walls, also wall and stairs up the slope to the round tower on the south side.

A new octagon turret to the Devil's tower has been built. ...

The Lancaster tower, containing six stories, and 100 feet high.

King George the Fourth's gateway.

The York tower, containing six stories, and 100 feet high.

The line of building extending to the south-east tower has been repaired, and raised an additional story, 200 feet, exclusive of towers.

The top part of the south-east or King's tower, which, with the corbels and battlements, required full 1,000 tons of stone; there were also five stories of windows, with stone-tracery inserted in this tower.

The library or Chester tower has been rebuilt, and is five stories high. ...

Many of the cross-walls betwixt the towers from the Devil's tower to the last-named tower at the north- east angle are new, and others have been raised to form servants apartments for the length of 380 feet, having new timbers and floors. ...

The Brunswick tower, upwards of 100 feet high and 40 feet in diameter, containing seven stories, has been entirely rebuilt.

The King's passage on the north side, and the great window, and George the Third's tower at the end of the ball-room, are entirely new.

There have been new windows with tracery inserted in the throne-room, presence-chamber, and state drawing-room; the walls over this last room have been carried up to form King George the Fourth's tower."

As so often happens with building projects, Wyatville went significantly over budget and was called upon to explain how that happened. His answer was both very believable and very disturbing: "The estimate was made when the King was residing in the Castle. I could not go and strip the apartments to see the walls and the timbers when the King was there, and therefore they were calculated as any person might do a probable expense. When the King retired, and I stripped the walls, the timbers were all found rotten, and necessarily the whole of the floors were removed…and the roof was in an equally bad state, and obliged to be taken off also, and many of the walls were cracked through, and many holes had been cut in, the Castle having been divided into different residences…it was very much dilapidated by each inhabitant cutting closets and cutting through the walls without any regard to the destruction of it. Then when the roof was removed, as there were not sufficient rooms for the King's servants, advantage was taken to put the roof higher, and make another story over, which of course would increase the estimate. The foundations in many instances were very bad; I was obliged to go 12 or 14 feet down, when I did not expect to go two: in one instance I went 25 feet down in the foundation; in another 30…Every place I opened was the same. The other day I had some of the timbers opened of the state apartments, and a man brought me a basket of rotten wood down from the timbers."

As it turned out, Queen Victoria would benefit from her uncle's efforts far longer than he ever did. Early in their marriage, she and her beloved husband, Prince Albert, made Windsor their primary home. With railroad lines and steamships along the Thames connecting them to London, they were able to host a wide variety of guests from around the nation and the world, and while the queen was very concerned regarding how the castle was run, she didn't feel any particular desire to change or update its buildings.

Colin Smith's picture of the statue of Victoria at Windsor Castle

The changes Victoria did make were primarily for show and comfort in the Upper Ward, including a new chapel built for their family's private use. This was significant because both the queen and her husband were very devout Protestant Christians and were determined to make sure their children were as well. Albert was all but obsessed with protecting their children from the wrong sort of influences, and in 1848 he persuaded Parliament to pass the Windsor Castle Act, which ordered that local streets that had previously passed through the castle grounds would instead be re-routed around them. This gave Victoria and Albert a larger area to enclose for their private use.

Albert

The State Dining Room had to repaired after it was damaged by fire in 1853, and in the Lower Ward, Prince Albert ordered stairs built so that he could more easily access the town of Windsor below. He also oversaw the installation of indoor plumbing in the castle for the first time in its history. Victoria also ordered that the Norman Gatehouse be closed to public use and made into a home for her loyal Private Secretary, Sir Henry Ponsonby.

After Albert died in the Blue Room in 1861, Victoria was so stricken with grief that she kept every aspect of the castle the same as it had been during his lifetime. She withdrew into its rooms physically just as she withdrew emotionally, leading Rudyard Kipling to style her the "Widow at Windsor."

The one area that became most important to her was the Albert Memorial Chapel, which she devoted herself to building. It was designed to reassure her of his secure afterlife and to assure her that they would one day be reunited. According to one contemporary guidebook, "The figures and canopy, surmounted by a cross designed by Sir Gilbert Scott, and executed by Messrs. Poole, are beautifully inlaid with costly marbles lapis lazuli, porphyry, alabaster, malachite, &c…The bas-reliefs, in panels, are in Sicilian marble, executed by Baron Triqueti.

The centre one represents the Resurrection; the one on the right, an Angel embracing the Cross; and on the left hand, Uplifting of the Sacramental Cup. The Altar Table consists of a grand slab of Levanto marble. At the front are three wreaths carved in boxwood; the right hand side is a Phoenix; in the centre a Lamb; and on the left the Pelican feeding its Young with its own Blood."

Upon ascending the throne, Edward VII came out from behind his mother's figurative shadow, and he was determined to also leave behind the literal shadows that the gloomy rooms in Windsor Castle cast. In his biography, *Edward VII: The Last Victorian King*, Christopher Hibbert wrote that "he strode about with his hat on his head, his dog trotting after him, a walking stick in his hand, a cigar in his mouth, giving orders; peering into cabinets; ransacking drawers; clearing rooms formerly used by the Prince Consort and not touched since his death; dispatching case-loads of relics and ornaments to a special room in the Round Tower ... destroying statues and busts of John Brown ... throwing out hundreds of 'rubbishy old coloured photographs' and useless bric-a-brac; setting inventory clerks to work at listing the cluttered accumulations of half a century; rearranging pictures."

Edward VII

Edward had waited a long time for the power to control his own life, and he wasted no time in modernizing the castle. Victoria had avoided putting gaslight in parts of the castle she frequented, preferring instead to continue to light the rooms with candles; Edward had electric lighting installed throughout the castle, and also added telephones. Victoria had been fine with the drafty castle being heated by fireplaces and coal stoves; Edward replaced the black coal stoves with central heating and ordered the barns converted to garages to house his automobiles.

Edward's son, George V, kept up the work during his reign, focusing his attention on modernizing the royal residence while his wife, the formidable Queen Mary of Teck, devoted herself to restoring the castle's interior glory. They both agreed that everything at the castle had to be the best that the country could produce, seeing their home as representing all that was good about English life. No doubt his act of highest devotion came in 1917 when, toward the end of World War I, as anti-German feeling was at his height, the king changed his family name from Saxe-Coburg-Gotha to Windsor.

When George VI succeeded his brother to the throne, he also chose to make Windsor his family home, and it was there that Queen Elizabeth II grew up. World War II and all the chaos it entailed, not to mention rationing, prevented him from making any significant improvements to the castle; instead, the Castle became once more a fortress against the enemy, as much of the London staff and the two princesses moved there for safety. The king and queen also slept there at night, spending their days in war torn London. The crown ordered that blackout curtains be installed over its beautiful windows, and that the most famous works of art be put into storage. As such, the basement was used to store the Crown Jewels.

Princess Elizabeth grew up and ascended to the throne in 1952, and though she and her family would live in London, they liked to retire to Windsor for the weekends. As a result, the castle was again properly updated with every modern convenience. However, having the Royal Family residing there, even part time, took its toll, as did the passage of time and the ever-increasing vibrations caused by traffic and aircraft. In March 1988, the *European Stars and Stripes* reported, "Round Tower at Windsor Castle...has been damaged by shifting foundations.... 'There has been a slight movement to the Round Tower al Windsor Castle. We are looking into it,' the government department said in a brief statement. 'The cause we do not yet know. There will be a report and that will contain what remedial action will need to be taken,' it added."

The coronation portrait of Queen Elizabeth

The report also noted that "the Daily Telegraph, which first broke the story, described the damage to the crenelated five story tower as serious following a shift in its ancient foundations. The London newspaper said the tower moved two weeks ago, bringing down plaster, causing cracks to appear in the stonework and jamming a door and two windows, h said the queen had inspected the tower."

In fact, the problem led to extensive work being done on the Upper Ward beginning in 1988, but that work was hardly completed before a tragedy struck the ancient castle when a fire broke out on November 21, 1992. To make matters worse, it appeared that the renovations themselves might have caused the blaze, or at least been partially to blame; it was later determined that a spotlight left too close to a 30 foot tall curtain ignited the blaze, which in turn spread quickly to other rooms in the State Apartments. Workers tried to put the blaze out with handheld fire extinguishers as they awaited the arrival of the local fire department.

In the wake of the costly fire, the *Associated Press* reported, "A stubborn, smoky fire at Windsor Castle on Friday damaged a private chapel, injured at least one person and threatened valuable works of art.... Authorities said damage was confined to a small portion of the sprawling castle. Soldiers and workers scrambled to carry paintings and other priceless objects from nearby state apartments."

The article went on to quote Prince Andrew, who was staying at the castle at the time of the fire: "It was the most extraordinary sensation. The castle looked like a giant chimney with flames, 60 to 70 feet billowing into the sky. It seemed as if nine centuries of history was going up in smoke...I have been in and looked in St. George's Hall and seen firsthand what it looks like, and it is a pretty nasty mess."

The article continued, "Hoses snaked from hydrants through the streets of Windsor to the hilltop castle along the River Thames, 20 miles west of London. The ceremonial courtyard inside...was strewn with firefighting equipment. More than 120 firefighters and 20 fire engines were on the scene. The fire, reported at 11:37 a.m., was declared under control but still not extinguished three hours later."

In fact, the fire was the worst in England in more than 20 years. According to Malcolm Bailey of the Royal Berkshire Fire and Rescue Service, who spoke several hours after the fire began, "It's confined to the northeast corner of the upper ward of the castle. Within that section the fire is still burning but not out of control."

Once it was clear everyone was safe, people shifted their concerns to the many artistic treasure housed in the castle. Dickie Arbiter, an assistant press secretary, noted, "There are paintings, works of porcelain, statues, tapestries, suits of armor. There's so much in there that it is impossible to say what has been damaged."

The following day, the *AP* observed, "The fire brigade said the Brunswick Tower, the private chapel, the Crimson Drawing Room, the Chester Tower and the Star Chamber also were badly damaged. "It would appear that the main structure of the building has held up very well," said David Harper, Berkshire deputy chief fire officer. Harper said several witnesses agreed that the fire was first noticed late Friday (November 21) morning in some curtains in a private chapel, an area where workmen were preparing for renovations...But it appeared the damage to one of the world's richest art collections might not be too extensive. Many items were removed from the castle by a human chain comprising staff, soldiers and Prince Andrew, the queen's second son, who was at the castle when the fire broke out before noon Friday. Heritage Secretary Peter Brooke said the cause of the fire was under investigation."

In fact, thanks to a bucket brigade consisting of castle employees, townsfolk, and even Prince Andrew himself, most of the valuables were removed from the rooms before the flames could reach them. Arbiter explained, "Prince Andrew was the first on the scene. Being a military officer, he knew how to take charge, and having grown up in the castle, he also knew where the irreplaceable treasures of the Royal Collection were. The staff and volunteers formed a human chain, passing the priceless manuscripts, smaller paintings, and centuries-old porcelain down the line to safety…Certainly all the paintings in the hall would have been lost forever, except this section was being rewired and a fire detector was being installed. Most of the Royal Collection in this area had been removed, except for three items: a portrait of George III, which was so large it couldn't betaken off the wall, a very heavy sideboard, and the organ. All three were destroyed."

It only took a little while before people were pointing fingers in an effort to hold someone responsible for the blaze, and for paying to restore the castle. In May 1993, the *Canadian Press* reported, "Allegations that officials 'ignored' warnings about Windsor Castle's fire protection system marked angry charges In Parliament and a stiff denial from Buckingham Palace Wednesday. London's *Today* newspaper said that a leaked report by the Berkshire Fire Service, which responded to a damaging blaze at the castle last November, warned officials of problems at the royal residence throughout the 1980s. Under the headline, 'Windsor Castle Fire Sensation,' *Today* said the fire service's recommendation to install castle fire alarms in the mid- 1980s was 'ignored' for years."

The article continued, "Other newspapers reported Wednesday that the fire was turned into a disaster by a series of blunders…. Blunders allegedly included staff dialing the castle's switchboard, instead of using the fire alarm system to warn of the blaze, and a 75-minute delay in bringing on line an auxiliary water pump…The newspapers' claims threatened to anger taxpayers already annoyed that they — not the Queen - will pay the lion's share for repairing her favorite residence, west of London. In 1991, Buckingham Palace took over control of Windsor Castle from the Property Services Agency, a government body. A spokesman for Buckingham Palace said Wednesday the newspapers made allegations not contained in the palace's copy of the fire service report. He said the fire report says the delay in the auxiliary pump had no significant effect on the fire-fighting effort last November."

Speaking on behalf of the taxpayers, the Member of Parliament for Bradford, in northern England, complained, "The government have been complacent and indifferent and now are calling on taxpayers to foot a massive bill. They should tell the Queen quite clearly that it is her responsibility to foot the entire bill."

The damage was extensive, too much for even a queen to write a check to cover. The brick and stone walls stood, but ceilings fell and rooms were gutted on all fixtures that weren't stone. St. George's Hall, the Crimson Drawing Room, the Green Drawing Room, and the Queen's Private Chapel were also severely damaged, as were the State Dining Room and the Grand Reception Room. Of the more than 100 rooms affected by fire and smoke damage, most were small and less well known. These included the Brunswick Tower, Chester Tower, Cornwall Tower, Great Kitchen, Holbein Room Prince of Wales Tower, Octagon Room, and Star Chamber.

The restoration work took years, with Prince Charles later noting, "Many of the workers had to learn unfamiliar skills to restore the ancient wood and glasswork. It's a testimony to their love, skill, and dedication that the results are so spectacular." *The Christian Science Monitor* reported in 1997, "While the castle was still smoking, restoration, archaeology, and architectural specialists were inspecting the damage. The committee decided to restore, but knowing the last restoration was in 1820, they needed the addition of modern improvements. Also, the extra space near the private chapel would become the new Lantern Lobby. According to Arbiter, 'The Lantern Lobby supplies the 'wow!' factor. Everyone who has seen it gazes around, and the first word out of his mouth is, 'Wow!'"

In fact, the queen raised most of the funds to restore her treasured home, as *The Christian Science Monitor* article observed: "It was 70 percent financed by entry revenue from opening sections of Buckingham Palace to the public, and now Windsor Castle, and 30 percent from the government's Grant and Aid Fund for the upkeep of the occupied royal palaces. The restoration, a shade over $60 million, came in several months ahead of schedule."

Thanks to the fire, and the need to raise money to make the repairs, Windsor Castle was once again opened to the public, and *The Christian Science Monitor* was able to tell readers that those visiting "will be able to view the restored Green and Crimson Drawing Rooms with the floor-to-ceiling bookcases and the intricate marquetry flooring, along with the elegant Octagon Anteroom and the amazing St. George's Hall. These four areas are indistinguishable from before the fire."

Today, in the second decade of the 21st century, Windsor Castle provides work for more than 500 people and hosts as many as a million tourists each year. It is also keeping up with the times by becoming more "green," with much of its power coming from two water turbines installed in the Thames. The crown is currently in the process of adding a visitor center and learning center to the grounds to make it both more tourist and school friendly.

Online Resources

Other books about English history by Charles River Editors

Other books about Windsor Castle on Amazon

Bibliography

Bickham, George. (1753) Deliciæ Britannicæ; or, the Curiosities of Kensington, Hampton Court, and Windsor Castle, Delineated. London: Owen.

Brindle, Steven and Kerr, Brian. (1997) Windsor Revealed: New Light on the History of the Castle. London: English Heritage.

Dixon, William Hepworth. (1880) Royal Windsor, Volume IV. London: Hurst and Blackett. OCLC 455329771.

Hibbert, Christopher. (2007) Edward VII: The Last Victorian King. New York: Palgrave Macmillan.

Mackworth-Young, Robin. (1992) The History and Treasures of Windsor Castle. Andover, UK: Pitkin.

Munby, Julian; Barber, Richard and Brown, Richard. (eds) (2007) Edward III's Round Table at Windsor. Woodbridge, UK: Boydell.

Nicolson, Adam. (1997) Restoration: The Rebuilding of Windsor Castle. London: Michael Joseph.

Pote, Joseph. (1755) Les Delices de Windsore: or, a Description of Windsor Castle and the Country Adjacent. Eton: Joseph and Thomas Pote.

Ritchie, Leitch. (1840) Windsor Castle, and Its Environs. London: Longman.

Robinson, John Martin. (2010) Windsor Castle: the Official Illustrated History. London: Royal Collection Publications.

Rowse, Alfred Leslie. (1974) Windsor Castle in the History of the Nation. London: Book Club Associates.

South, Raymond. (1977) The Book of Windsor. Chesham, UK: Barracuda Books.

Tighe, Robert Richard and Davis, James Edward. (1858) Annals of Windsor, Being a History of the Castle and Town, with some Account of Eton and Places Adjacent, Volume II. London: Longman.

Free Books by Charles River Editors

We have brand new titles available for free most days of the week. To see which of our titles are currently free, click on this link.

Discounted Books by Charles River Editors

We have titles at a discount price of just 99 cents everyday. To see which of our titles are currently 99 cents, click on this link.

Made in the USA
Middletown, DE
10 April 2019